In these poems I'm remembering
some of those I have loved:
ones who have gone
and those who remain in
mind and heart, loved, forever

Naked L♡ve Tokens

122 poems - 38 illustrations

Pamela Blanchfield

These poems are memories and thoughts

of life and loves, both past and present,

recalled sometimes with sadness, yet also

with the hope of future dreams and desires.

All have been written in the last five months

and without the appearance of my muse –

the one who untied my wings,

would never have flown out

I am thanking you, again,

with words and love, always

Contents

Echoes in the meadow

Love Token

Words you don't want to say

Are they too few

Always unspoken

Left somewhere silently

Unspent love token

Things you would like to say

But never can do

Places recalled back when

Special for just one

By one now spoken

Left somewhere silently

Unspent love token

Not buried or left back then

Desires that never have gone

You know your words could kill

So hold back please

Leave it unspoken

Safe somewhere silently

Unspent love token

Words that could give life or -

Silence guarantees

Know

Know if I saw you right now
I would want to say so much,
Look once more into your eyes
Ask you why it is, and how
I'm still craving that same touch,
Yes, true, I'm foolish not wise

Know if I saw you right now
I'd so want to hear your voice,
Look long again at your face
Forget anything I know,
My will would be left no choice,
Dreams found in my secret space

Wonder if you saw me today
Would you even need to speak?
A latent flash in my eyes
Spark of things we don't need to say?
Could we be close - heart to cheek?
Would something be recognised?

And if you saw me today,

Would you let me softly show

Loving ways I always feel,

Not in any words I say,

Could we briefly pause, lightly go

Where our souls could then reveal?

Then if you later said talk,

Tell me what makes you so sad?

You know well my heart is blue,

I'd say I missed our lifetime walk:

Life and lives unknown, never had

Down that road not walked with you

Avenues of Love

Turned my back often, the other way
Once I had finished exploring,
Or met crazy or lightweight or gay
Occasionally just utterly boring

Time is past so suppose I'll admit
Occasions knew I'd caused tears,
But some parts never can fit
Even after many long years

Oh I've been stupid I well know,
Advantage was clearly elsewhere
Which battered my spirit so low,
When some were too selfish to care

Avenues of love where we wander
Feeling lost and the smaller part,
Youthful idiocy to squander,
Squashed, mud splattered love heart

But one turned his broad back on me,

Broken harsh years left to find

I'd hidden him as deep as could be

Yet today he still lives in my mind

Truth is painful to see clearly,

But older and wiser we can see

That the one we wanted most dearly

Turned yet stayed permanently

Almost

In yesterday's far realm unexplored

Glittered a fire green-gold morning,

Sky cornflower marigold dawning,

Time found that treasure-word hoard

In a lost land of beauty, yet still flawed

By an ancient unheeded heart warning

Memory in submerged waves, but for one,

Vestige of visions lie there, trace my soul,

Haunted imperfection time swiftly stole

Wide landscapes once wandered, now gone,

Crystal cloudburst rained then sun shone

On resting fragments made almost whole

How Do You Lay?

Do you lay side by side in a place of calm

Or feel your soul hounded by rising alarm?

Do you hear a slow scream build to a roaring shout

That stays trapped within never getting out?

Do you lay close while wandering miles away?

Talking words inside you never can say?

In relaxation do you have what you dreamt?

Or has long familiarity bred contempt?

Are the souls of your drowsing all kind and wise?

Or do you chase visions then tell yourself lies,

Maybe you smile and slip off to a happy land

Where stars shine twinkling on gold endless sand,

Dazzling sunshine rays never turn to thunder,

How do you lay? I wonder, I wonder

I Kept Some Love (for G)

Two together appeared way back then
But I was allowed to choose only one,
Two appealing, both interesting men,
Blind old road veered ahead, very long

Had to stop, think hard, then somehow choose,
Find a way I could make up my mind,
One would turn away, one love I'd lose,
The answer wasn't easy to find

One was tender, clever, kissed with soft lips
Had a kind heart which made me fonder,
But like me – too like me, knew he'd soon trip
And his bright roving eye would then wander

So I chose the one with hard words that cut
Knowing he'd always put himself first,
Though I ploughed the furrows he stayed in a rut,
Years made me wonder if I'd chosen worst

You parted that day with those words, years ago

We'd always gelled, had such easy fun,

My heart now is heavy, hearing you're low

I kept some love inside, shaded by sun

I can only return it now with much more,

Though aware today it's a different kind,

None of us can see what life has in store,

The peace I'm sending I do hope you'll find

Shorter days - I pause here in reflection,

Boulders, puddles – and carry a heavy load,

That way was unmarked - obscured direction

That once had a sharp divide in the road

Your Pale Face (for N)

I always kept that little thing,

Orange man in his hiding place

Reminded me we used to sing,

That lovely vision – your pale face,

Now he is lost, that funny man,

Words come from you again today,

Memories, take me way back when

Young us recalling yesterday,

Adorable perfect young guy,

Dreams desires swift hard forsaken,

And only one real reason why

You had already been taken!

Remembering Rog

Periwinkle blue matching the sky today,

Rippling stream echoes like your light lost laugh,

Poppies red, petals drift, blowing away,

I didn't see then the wheat from the chaff,

Gentle in kindness, jokes and shy smile,

Your long far-distant lost lonely trial

I was stupid and somewhere else that night,

Why wasn't I really quite there to hear?

I didn't detect your serious sad plight,

Too far away as you called out so near,

You spoke soft, a quiet but heartfelt need,

Your heart screamed low and I just didn't heed

Buttercups yellow are blazing this year

Gold memory lingers long with regret,

I see your lovely face often, and so clear,

My failure to you I could never forget,

Dandelion clocks to the breeze light seeds send,

And you died alone that night my dear friend

My Twin Hedonist

Instant attraction undeniable:

Seven years younger than I,

Boundaries so soon were pliable

We lit fire sparks in each other's eye

Yes we met up in secret loving trysts

Crazed kindred spirits of lust,

Smoking and loving back in the mists

Doing exactly what we knew we must

Your long lovely hair and wonderful nose,

Yes, the part I almost – loved best,

Alive set on fire we always rose,

But also put each other to the test

Your young body, a delight and hot thrill,

My twin hedonist of our youth,

And here I'm remembering you still,

Your light laugh and the eventual truth

In passion later on we were crazy,

Could have died when I fell off the bed,

In caring though think we got lazy

Then we punished each other instead

We'd tumble together and with joy scream,

Couldn't get enough on some nights,

Hot funky love's wet passionate dream

Until we had our harsh verbal fights

One time we'd love hard then next we'd hate,

Our attraction grew into pain,

Maybe too alike to truly relate

And today – would it be just the same?

You worked hard, were very clever and smart,

Had demons but angels there as well,

Wild fun was had – I'd say, hand on heart -

Would this be the same tale you'd also tell?

Your Light

You were never the best-looking guy
But your light always filled up the space
Mischief and fun wreathed your face
I saw you that day, passing by,
Smiling you spoke your young words:
The best chat up lines that I'd heard

Yes, your grandfather fancied me,
Your father tried to entice me too
Both I liked, but best by far you,
Dark waves and your heart running free,
So I joined you a while in the fast race
Summer - that look of hot joy on your face

I know we are related with our blood
And some would have called it taboo
But they didn't know me, or you
So could never have understood
Our short fusion high there in the park
Collisions too wild after dark

I saw you then in Muswell Hill,

Road where my grandfather had lived,

He died of malnutrition,

And my crazy love damped our ignition,

We walked that day in the great park,

Got stoned and drunk, had sex after dark

Why did we get so fast and far out?

We could have stayed in - just had more fun,

Then that late night, so many beers,

Your distance and hatred of tears,

Do you too recall our young fast fling,

When lust crowned the queen and the king?

Attraction

Along drifts on forget-me-not pathway
Same blue as your jacket and lustrous eyes,
Always gentle with no need for fake lies
Attraction was mutual, so bound our ties
Took us floating far to another day
Until that sad and unwelcome surprise

It was easy to relate and much more,
Think of your pixie's pointy shoes and sway,
Shy smile and laugh as you swept in the door,
Know that others often thought you were gay
Which didn't matter to me anyway,
And you could drink them all on to the floor

Cute but you had a big booze appetite,
Certainly drank lots I vividly recall,
Legendary intake though remained upright,
And in one way were anything but small,
Loved women and knew just how to enthral,
We had loving, perfect passionate nights

And smoothly was the way we tuned in where

Both candid, our honesty not concealed,

And you loved with a pure passion so rare,

Glamour for you always so much appealed,

Gentle love built between us then revealed

We took it too far till we were forced to care

Cool, contained calm composure, so like mine,

Feet and heeled boots really turned you on,

Pale blue your bright eyes so often would shine,

Together we so well-fitted, belonged

Jigsaw pieces - we easily got along,

Until fate's cracked harsh bell rang on our time

Stamina undoubted, subtle power,

There was always that deep, marked attraction

Immediate at your late arrival hour,

Quiet, then guaranteed satisfaction

Fused in our easy loving reaction,

Couldn't imagine sweet turning to sour

Crowd at the bar - we'd not met for a while
Like magnets both felt the same instant buzz:
No words needed, just that same knowing smile,
Connection, our way, unspoken because
We always knew the right route to find us,
Brewed a storm with no escape or denial

Untamed - glorious: got together quite late,
Recall how we quenched each other's long thirst,
Higher after months, instant way to relate
Never knew we were creating the worst,
Only remember that night, peaks so great,
How quickly our leisure would be reversed

Think of you now, special, though time has flown
Like birds on forget-me-not way – fast-scared,
Saw you later, survivor, lived alone,
Such pleasure denied which should have been shared,
We matched so well though not so much with words,
Pity no one else found with you what we'd known

Do You

Your thoughts are a secret

And mine almost an open book,

Heart written on a page,

Do you ever think if you could return

You'd take a much closer look -

At us in a younger age?

My dreams aren't a secret,

My library though is bare,

Do you ever linger lost

Hear strange words rise in space,

Wonder how you got there,

And maybe what it's cost?

Do you want to share a secret?

Know I could do that too

But I wonder now, are you near

Or somewhere very far from this

Perhaps quite crazy view

Where you once again appear

Memory Steps

Think I laughed to hear of your heart's desire:
Wish for a warm woolly jumper feeling
How could I have dreamed how time would transpire?
Hot roads and highs my wild ways were stealing,
Your dreams of the one you'd choose to be near,
I had no thought of cold future day tears

Younger, but somehow you were much more wise,
And I couldn't see then your prescience,
Blinkered, my captured kaleidoscope eyes,
Coloured love vision without common sense,
Sweeping illusion had cast a dense veil
Or comprehension of what makes love fail

North West autumn cooler breezes blowing

On that same wide road, so much later now,

Those days just one knew where they were going,

Ingrained memory steps trodden long ago,

Us laughing together, walking there then

Wish I could retrace – I'd not laugh again

Hope the genie sprinkled you with her charms:

Have you weathered winters with a warmed heart?

Are you held close, cherished in caring arms?

Been well-understood to nourish your art?

Kept protected by love's fire to chase chill?

My naked rebel soul wonders this still

If

And had I been of more interest

In our far blown younger lives

Could we then have manifest

Found for each other more sparks to thrive?

Together taken a brilliant ride

Discovered things life has perhaps denied,

Brought out with loving the mutual best?

Could I have lived a much cleaner life?

Brought smiles to both our faces?

Without that label called wife,

Reached undiscovered unknown places?

Run in more worthwhile happier races?

Found all the lost missing aces?

Smoothed out harsh cold currents of strife?

Could you have grown more true and sincere?

If I'd been long-time with you?

Through forests where green joys appear,

Could you have seen a higher view?

Success deserved, a straighter way through,

Had a great life for you and me too?

Just old questions I'm pondering here...

But then maybe you've had perfection,

Doubtful you'd tell anyway,

Here as I pause in reflection

Thinking of things we never did say,

Dreams unlived – yes, mine - just dust today,

Years and those songs never heard you play -

But only I miss that connection

Yes I felt the soft butterfly land
Kiss of creative flown then,
Glimpsed the escaped unknown strand,
Know myths I'll recall once again,
Symphonies of the heart and pen,
A time breezes took wings away when
I just couldn't hold onto your hand

Were we always two opposing sides?
Some battle I failed to see,
Forces destined to divide,
Now I know some things aren't meant to be,
Traits and manners played elusively -
Did you trap me once, then set me free
But leave bitter crumbs for me to find?

Preferred lovely times when I believed
Mind's tales - fairy stories told –
Desires yet to be achieved,
Glittering spirits dancing in gold,
Welcoming words to warmly enfold
Opaque love endearments spoken bold,
My soul was happy then, undeceived

White Dove

Do I call it sorrow of the sight-afflicted?

Heart in denial but know I'm still addicted,

Since I made a mind-dam when the floods burst,

Arid years yet now find a much greater thirst,

What is the low whispering of the name?

Spirit-teaser which gives no certain end game

Yet love looks ever-hopeful for best not worst.

Do I call it destined soul damnation?

White dove that scratched life into creation,

Words for the foolish or lines of the wise,

Truth of how we survive and tell ourselves lies,

Attempt to bury our losses and fear

Till they rise screaming again after years,

Love can't close our hearts but will cover our eyes

Buried Treasure

When the world was spinning crazy, too fast

Running, we missed each other's worth and truth,

Urgency of wild dizzy thoughtless youth,

Holding then breaking apart not to last

Unveiled shadows later which time had cast

Whirlwind of joy our love was so fleeting,

A blink in years spent apart forever,

Left undiscovered gold buried treasure,

Yet years later our kindred minds meeting,

Views seen of wrong turns, loss, late soul-greeting

Revealed – though we can't make a revision,

Heartbreak of being deprived, lost then wise,

Blinkered way back, now unmasked saddened eyes,

Life lines - daggers of today's division,

Tears lament unexplored fated collision

You Led Me

You led me into the orchard
Words ripened on mystery's breeze,
Blew through the torn years and found me
Sat alone sad, under the trees

Harvest fruit, maybe a vintage,
Ripened by cracked suns and cold moons,
Scratched beneath skin, spilled a truth pledge,
You bowed low to another tune

Bright and dark – a gathering up -
Core secrets stored in my being,
Blossom flowered, not bright enough,
Demeter long-tied, now seeing

You always know where you'll find me,
Tumbling words match rhymes fast spinning,
Lines released but not flying free,
Born from a riven beginning

Not Long Ago

Not long ago in the dazzling dream minutes
Bright meadow filled with myriad blooms,
A fragrant soft corner sweet, you and me in it,
I listened to your voice and your beloved tunes

It was really only a lime verdant yesterday
Sun, orange wild skies, a winter warm feeling
Purely created by the words you would say,
With heart music – roused desires, so appealing

Under dappled trees think we lingered a while,
Tasted harmony when our minds united,
Stirred my lost hours where I matched your smile,
Tomorrow's shadow dawned when I wasn't invited

Mysteries linger and questions long remain,
Wonder about hiding places there in your mind,
Conversations lamented, music's lost refrain,
Absence and silence and you - always undefined

I didn't spot the steep drop over the cliff side,

Believed in future magenta fun fusion,

Now the puzzle left for me is how I must hide

And escape from my much-missed illusion

But I return to the rustle in tall green woods

Searching for magic perfume that disappeared,

See it flying from memory's strange falsehood

Through a tangled route that never quite clears

Love can turn from rose to black bitter, I know,

A bereavement felt without blank death,

But when feelings inside just never quite go,

You still crave a warm touch and feel of that breath

Now I have a battle to fight, so unexpected,

What is left, can I call on philosophy?

Alone today but no longer protected,

With my disbelief, was it not meant to be?

Can't deny I have had times with hard feelings,
Encroaching deep space you've left behind
Where we had friendship and joy in our dealings,
Do know with you that in some ways I am blind

I never want to replace love hearts with hate
Though struggle, left low with loss and defeat,
Within thoughts can't find help, so must create
Still, a brighter place where our souls might meet

And if I ever see you once more in this blue span
Will I be reminded of love as I look in your eyes?
Or a circle ever turning where this all began
And a battle fought by fools with loving lies?

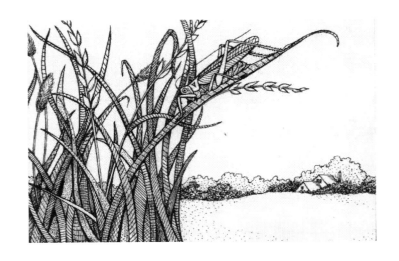

Footsteps in the meadow

Like Wine...

Some men are like the finest of wine
As time passes they age and mature,
Character is pronounced all the more,
Rough notes converted to ones refined,
Greatly redeemed from what went before

Subtle, polished piquant, soft each sip:
Strands of mulberry, lime and plum fruit,
Mellowed surprise from young notes acute,
Tastes linger, reborn skin, flesh and pip,
Wisdom gained, full-bodied, absolute

Some wines sadly lack though, like some men,

Fake, without fruit, just added bubbles,

With headaches, a sour taste and troubles,

Mundane - no balance found even when

Tasted twice, the harshness then doubles

If you've sampled finest vintage wine

Give fair chance to a new or old one,

Years pass but sharp defects may live on,

Don't assume age will transform to fine

Men are like sour grapes, label some anon.

Stolen

Ostrich I still see you alone there
But always minus your head
And crazy that backwards tread,
Were you thrown by a spirit-scare,
Stolen by someone, you said,
But I can see a bump in the sand
Well, I think there's some lost thread,
Who could possibly understand
Where this long shoreline has led?
Perhaps extend a helping hand
Guide you now to look in the light,
Remember the way you once fought
Lessons you thought life had taught
When you knew wrong and right?
That was before you saw the wild sea
Glittering and howling back when
The tide ran out but didn't return
That day that turned so swiftly night,

Yes I recall the time and the key

That knife has strangely twisted again

Interval that was calm and clear

But it was so lovely back then

When the soul essence came near

Your head was wearing that smile,

Hidden now, and for some while

Waiting for the tide to re-appear,

Well it's dry down there, you're alone

You mustn't wait another year

Lift your head from what's futile,

Who really cares about your trial,

Send dreams off to be wind-blown,

Ask why they are worthwhile?

They are dead the seeds that you've sown

Now raise your head in sad denial

Endings

I must have had this coming
I left so many hearts broken
Words gentle to end the loving
Invariably by me always spoken

I should have worked this one out
Before black day left me wanting more
With love unspent, life hours left wishing
Picking myself and my heart off the floor

Yes I am sorry for those sad endings
One loves more – the way things turn out,
So if retribution was once in hiding
It visited me too and left no doubt

This Scar

How long will it take to heal this scar?

I'm not talking about on my flesh,

Jagged line running inside, too far

Heart symbol tied up in wire mesh,

It had almost healed over too,

At least, I told myself that then,

But when you came back in view

Knew I'd lied once more again,

But I think it was well-concealed,

Been that way some long while,

Then you re-appeared, revealed

New old sad tears after my smile,

Surprise - you came back in my life,

Felt complete through winter's cold,

Now you've left my heart with this knife

Wounded much like the past foretold,

My reason tries to make some sense,

Way that I strangely feel about you,

Years now and it's more intense

I'm today and yesterday's fool

The Perfect Place

The internet is a perfect place

For the disingenuous

To link and creep with a light trace

Showing the world a lying face

Clothed in webs of splintered lace

Hiding faking unknown grace

False images displayed in vanity's race

Liking and loving avoiding disgrace

Superficial word embrace

Last week's love easy to erase

Send to silent cyber space

Truth and honesty to debase

Phony ego to showcase

True emotions to efface

Friends the strangers interface

To disabuse and to debase

Say it loud in upper case

Futile pursuit imagined chase

Motives masked and misplaced

Coward's holy coup de grace

So for those with a lying face

The internet is the perfect place

Narcissus

Cowards can't cut the mustard

Reality cringing under the hedge

With a heart as yellow as custard

Selfish worn wobbling pledge

Slightly hot but with a bitter edge

Gaze long admire that reflection

Some delusion in glory vain

Shallow wordless defection

Ride that merry-go-round again

Dark skies one day will bring rain

Delightful for that Narcissus

Endlessly searching his twin

Beware of the lost ones who kiss us

They only look without, not within

Another thrill is about to begin

Feint heart will never know true love

Apart from mirror games played alone

Keep the feather of the white dove

Stroke emotions that never have grown

Illusions once more to winds blown

Truth

Truth is the name that opens the doors

Paves our pathways with golden leaves

Truth talks with love

Knows well how to give

Sees transparent the human flaws

For lies it laments and greaves

Love will always return with much more

Rewards to quietly receive

Send truth with love

It's the only way

It's the secret told often before

Yet so obscured for some to believe

Your footstep

I'm trying to make you invisible
You're now becoming almost transparent,
Did you think my love was derisible?
Perhaps your absence makes that apparent

Your image is just slowly fading now
Well, until something once more hits my heart,
Maybe it's that same ancient knife you threw
When silence before spoke loudly, apart

I thought you were special, loving, so kind,
Different from the old ghost version of you,
Time evaporates those thoughts with no sign,
Twice, shadow man, you again were not true

I'm struggling to see your image fading
Traces hiding with lost love I still find,
Darkest corners still show tear-stained shading
Where you stamped your footstep deep in my mind

Island Memory

Then in reverse taking the long Irish road

Alongside the Atlantic fresh coast that glowed,

Out over the ancient peaty island, wild,

High mountains, clear rivers, gold moors, undefiled,

Travelling back home that far past summer day

Leaving life there continuing, a timeless way

Passing through saw a sign at a village hall:

Maybe just pick up something lovely, quite small,

A sale: local things to buy - doors open wide:

No harm to look, with some free time on our side,

Special curious place, and farthest point out west,

Thought perhaps I'd find a gift — see art expressed

There was seaweed, plants, pots of jam, cakes and tarts

Plus a kaleidoscope to plant in my heart,

I saw them in the corner quite suddenly,

Flowers grouped as bright as could possibly be:

The combination made my mind leap and sing -

There amongst other cute hand-made crafty things

I knew sadly I could not buy a bouquet,

But future garden schemes were reborn that day,

Mid-June heat would wilt blooms over such distance;

Yet memory stayed - lights up my existence

And I stood transfixed by their pure vibrancy,

Posy grown by a person that set me free

Orange, shock reds, magenta, purples, pink, white

Flowers placed together that just looked so right,

And hot cerise – yellow with cool shades of blue,

I planned to lift spirits I'd plant in that way too

Dizzy palettes with an old new direction,

All a riot of fabulous perfection

My gratitude goes to that gardener unknown,

So thanks always for special mind seeds you've sown

Glorious arrangement I couldn't keep that day,

That grew boldly into my new dazzling way,

Superb vividly mixed colour collision,

Such joy that formed then a fresh flower vision

Rules

'Don't walk on the grass'

Of course that's the path I'll choose,

Probably no one else will pass

And although your esteem I might lose

I really couldn't care,

If they say 'don't', know I will,

Well just stand, sniff and stare,

On your tidy righteous hill,

If it's out of bounds I'll go there,

Always was inside, this kink

Go on, give me another dare,

Broke many hard set rules

At eight I used to drink ink,

Laughed in the old church school,

Well, see if I really care

Not bothered what you think,

Forbidden pathways are mine,

You stand in the neat queue,

And look satisfied as you shine

Then watch me step out of line

And rattle your ordered view

Need to feel untethered

From ties and restriction

Out the rule book I threw,

At one with the fur and feathered

Always, this is nothing new,

Freedom is my conviction

Just a Memory

Didn't know that key was in my pocket

Or my picture in your locket

I was just passing through

Recall someone like you

Before I went to the meadows

Stopped to smell many flowers

I don't know where time goes

Or that I stole your hours

You were just a memory

Back in the last century

Left you there alone to be

Something unknown to me

Down there by the rushing sea

Way back in the last century

Now I can see that room

Smell again your perfume

I'd gone away to smell more flowers

Not aware I'd stolen your hours

Until I remembered your way

Thought I'd look you up again

Drift along and just say hi,

Voice from last century

You hadn't meant that much to me

Life's weird if you ask why

Just had liked what I could see

Didn't go beyond skin deep

Never even thought to try

Never knew of the shrine you'd keep

One in your heart to me

It was your heart it cost

Never thought that could be

Then I found for you what was lost

There in my pocket, the key

Don't Say!

Don't say I can only memorise

Lost echoes and those thrilling cries,

Mutual flesh, heated thighs,

Unions then, delighted sighs,

So clearly I can visualise

Moaning glorious gasping highs,

Some were just the perfect size,

But their minds were not the prize,

Youth's not about being wise,

Sometimes it's lust and loving lies

And wild desire in flashing eyes

Sizzling with red hot surprise,

Carnal passions in welcome ties

Rushing rivers without guise

Throbbing rhythm amplifies,

But is it only now I realise

However hard I might devise

Or need or want to make flames rise,

It's not the body's thirsty demise

Or that I don't still fantasise

But opportunity has minimised,

Or is it my allure to tantalise,

Maybe I don't much socialise

So now fail to fully optimise

Meet that free spirit to fraternise,

Light hot fires and synchronise,

Until the dark hour of no disguise

When time is one thing that defies

The thrill in mind that never dies

D

'D': simply the fourth letter and
One we are so used to seeing
Although think I now understand
It's wrapped itself in my being

'D': starts the lovely word delight
Enveloping when it drifts by,
Life ascends new dizzying heights:
Free of doubts, we don't reason why

'D': charming whispers of dreaming,
Butterflies in pink fantasy lands
Heart and mind blissful, seeming
To be held in sun-rainbow hands

'D' then captures deepest desire,
Furnace flaring wild at thought-touch,
Flaming delicious fire,
Passions that perhaps rouse too much

'D' sadly begins distance too,

Place where all the lonely ones stray,

Darker each vanished fading view,

Dim horizon dull dreary grey

'D', disaster of a love lost,

Bleak demon that will drain the soul,

The penalty price false dreams cost

Condemned to half and not a whole

'D' that dips hard into demise,

No mind wants to ever tread there

Admitting decisions unwise

As emptiness falls everywhere

'D' don't wish to know desertion,

Guaranteed to stir such unease,

Absence though makes the assertion,

Wide vast void where nothing can please

'D' begins the word devotion,

Beautiful, aimed in the right place,

But the saddest wave on the ocean

With no reciprocal smiling face

'D' yes - maybe I'm wearing that hat,

Some pointed joke from childhood days,

Dear D, I wonder about that:

Dreams devour my mind as it strays...

'D' – represents our destiny:

Long road where both fools and brave go,

Sealed door hiding life's mystery

Not for us to foretell or know

Days like These

Days like this, on black days

Doesn't matter if skies are blue

It's hard just to get through,

Pull up into a better view

Remember my light old ways

I was always the smiling one

With wisdom words for all,

Ready at their beck and call

Thought life could never stall,

Where has optimism gone?

Because here I am – feel lonely,

No I'm not here on my own,

But feel sure hope has flown

Ultimately know I am alone,

Dreams and wishes of if only

Know I gave others so much
I'm adrift with no kind words,
Irony strikes it's so absurd,
No sunbeam heart voice is heard
Or loving look or warm touch

So now here through this black day,
On desperation dark row,
There's one thing that I do know,
Want to look up, not below,
Somehow I need to find the way

Do others think I'm super strong
And so don't need their thought,
The solo warrior who's fought
And by some magic safely brought
Myself peace my whole life long?

Seems a fundamental lack

Washes me wide off the shore,

Kind words and joy heard no more

Just cold inner space to explore,

My soul feels under such attack

So the black dog growls at my door

A friendly cat would be preferred,

Softness my spirit perhaps stirred

Might have listened and cared,

The bark sounds harsher than before

Isolation

I saw such a beautiful deep wide place,

Possibilities, laughter and fun,

But almost before it had begun

I sank lower back in a lonely space

Where cloud obscured the much brighter sun,

And warmth vanished, leaving ice in its trace

Those moments wished for a lifetime ago

Which suddenly, re-joined, felt so near,

Unexpected the hero appeared

Sent me love, sure words life would happen so,

But then dense mists made dreams disappear

And doubt has replaced what I thought I'd know

You are hard lost in your isolation

Which leaves my heart in the same place too,

All you left is wild visions of you

With chill spikes of sharp separation,

Oppressive, impenetrable deep blue,

Made wordless, muse of my inspiration

I am down in a desolate deep place

And how far have you drifted from here,

My memory of times you were near

And long wish to again see your face

Stokes absence along with a cold fear

That only your presence can now replace

A Pirate

A pirate came one day
Only wanted tiny treasure
Moments for fun and leisure,
But he then took away
Peace and my pleasure

Arrived with a wild flash,
Couldn't catch that shine,
Left something behind
Planted a bold backlash
Jewelled within my mind

Diamonds didn't spark
Needed another gem beside
Life not thought or tried
Grounded lost landmark:
Sailed off on oceans wide

Years he sailed the world sea

While slow raindrops fell,

Now no words remain to tell

He ever gave thought to me

The pirate I still can't quell

Just a passing pirate's plunder

He stole logic - didn't know,

Gold seeds he didn't grow

To sow calm after thunder,

Many misty strange moons ago

For Some

For some attached men

The fun is in the flirting

Fickle fascination

Remote titillation

Passing preoccupation

Not about who they're hurting

For some attached men

It's a world of sexy fun

Skilled experts at teasing

They're only ever pleasing

Themselves, then seizing

The opportunity to run

For some attached men

Those who never plan to stray

Lovers of fast cheap thrills

Hot whims that moment fills

Until pure passion kills

Then they swiftly run away

For some attached men

Who boast they have big balls

But play games of old pretence

Relighting some drowned sense

Being men their only defence

When their dumb silence falls

For some attached men

Always faithful they might say

Other women can revive juices

Best virtue of their uses

So without further excuses

At distance in mind they stray

With some attached men

Passion's in their sticky grip

Turned on while they hide truth

Chasing elements of lost youth

Soon turn distant and aloof

The great thrill is in their ego trip

Snakes

Snakes swirl now into feared dust space,

Slithering, harsh, dry, once remote,

Pixel life – sings a perfect note,

Heart-pull, familiar much-missed face

Wished I'd been a bright bower bird,

Laid out jewels in silent love,

Why lament the lone white-grey dove?

Why cry for minor notes unheard?

Wished I'd adored you with flowers,

Covered you in kisses, more,

Danced a spirit overture,

Think I just met hungry hours

Before I carried rocks into space

Had I written you love in lines,

Would you have then called one more time?

Or still laughed in another place?

Starkly I face this soul abyss,

From renewed searing, sleeping truth,

Haunting regret rushing from youth

And one I'm sad I still miss

Mossed melancholy desire

And a wish that's grown these years,

But alone, wonder with fear

Will your return still transpire?

Don't

Don't stand high, look down and judge anyone
Our short days are mutually fast flying,
We must face truth - soon for all they'll be gone
Leaving ghost laughter echoes and crying

Don't criticise, always try to be kind,
Smile, reach out, breathe with love, forgo sighing,
Battles lived and fought in the heart and mind
Smooth for some, but others often trying

The road won't stretch for endless miles ahead,
Soon the horizon too-fast approaches
Use love always in what is thought and said,
Words of hate only the self reproaches

Don't ever resent what another's got,

We can't know their harvest or grains of truth,

Be content and at peace with your own lot

As sunset rushes towards us from youth

I won't be concerned with your opinion,

My bare feet feel dew as they touch green grass,

Your doctrines won't control my dominion,

Sunrise dawns brighter and swiftly clouds pass

We have different ways we think, live and be,

No two paths have flowers arranged the same,

Don't lock the gate, leave my heart and mind free

So I can run as winds whisper my name

This Year

Constant, I'm somehow always aware,
Feeling, know I don't want this to be there,
It's like my soul is laid wild and bare,
Across my heart is a deep dragging tear,
Because I'm not sure you'll still be there,
And inside, know too well that I care

But you are caught hard in cold places
With ghosts, dreams and laughing missed faces,
Watching tenderness switched to feint traces,
Missing the old life of soul embraces,
Hiding terrors inside the mind chases,
Fighting demons that loss replaces

It's a hard bridge on which I'm standing
Hoping soon for that heart-soft landing,
Unspoken but felt understanding,
Not cast back to that island, black stranding,
The joy your contact brought, then handing
A sad heart to dictate by commanding

Now you're lost, swept to uncertain tides

While passion's dulled and creation hides,

Spears that pierce fight sharp battles inside

Where now devils and darkness preside,

Bringing ocean tears endlessly cried,

But angels stay close – they're your guides

I'm not quite the fool my words may seem,

Battle of days with recurring theme,

Like salmon thrashing, swimming upstream,

Heading home to the place they can dream,

Perhaps I'm too honest, often extreme,

Or have you turned from the way in between?

Constant, this long wishing, harsh soul ache,

Are we victims of love dreams we make?

Mists and high illusions our mistake,

Shadows drift by and life can forsake,

Storms crash in, emotional earthquake

In this year of loss and bleakest heart break

For Dear Pete

Along a perfect avenue

My mind pauses in reflection:

Looking back, clearly see us two,

Our easy teenage perfection

Just around that sweeping wide bend

Wandering lanes under high trees

We made such a natural blend,

Exploring in untroubled ease

Laughter tinkles there, an echo,

Church – planned escape, we slipped away,

Where on Sundays we both would go

Still shine with bright blossom today

Alive our loving memory,

Resurrected in older minds,

Yet in your room, shadows will be

Connected together all time

And evenings, always - nine o clock

You'll hear a soft knock on the door,

A tray of tea, so we had to stop

But just wanted to continue for more

A rustle in leaves, placid words,

Old paths paved with patterns of joy,

But your Mum thought your viridian cords

Most unsuitable for her young boy!

And caring, at the bus stop you'd stay,

Till that night you gazed and you dreamed:

"A dress for our Miranda one day",

For me, no longer carefree, it seemed

And hope I wasn't cruel, unkind,

Because I heard, then sent my guitar

As you struggled somewhere with your mind,

Before destiny took you so far

I know laughter remains this long while,

Courage, art and trials, all despite,

I can hear you laugh, and see your smile

And gain strength from your spirit and fight

Breeze blows along a suburban way,

New footsteps now tread with ours too,

Our moments, alive there still today

With love and thanks I send now to you

The Perfect Box

Never did find the perfect box
Where all the pieces fit neatly in,
With one of those gold heart-shaped locks
Perfect items placed just-so within

I think I have heard about them
They live in lands where the fairies dwell
Jewelled lids with a glowing pink gem
Written inside a safe sacred spell

Secrets contained just for certain eyes
Tokens and trinkets, letters, much more
Life tucked therein with no sharp surprise
Life of smooth love all quite safely stored

Never found that special box, so rare
Know I have heard of them anyway,
Perhaps I did have one once, somewhere
Long ago, I've forgotten today

To Tom Sunbeam

Why do sunbeams get taken?

Rainbows dissolved in grey skies,

And lost in the wondering whys

Of a dark world, earthquake-shaken

Brightest beams shine much stronger,

Warmth and goodwill spreading wide,

Love shared, from deep life source, inside

Eternal, that lives on longer

Notes of high thrilling unison,

Words sometimes of pathos and pain,

Enduring memory, sounds soft strains

In our butterfly brief frisson

We fly and spread joy and delight,

Create colour - lift mind and eye,

But in defeat we're left asking why

Unasked, transformed, we're made to fight

Darkness can surround some hearts

Others reflect light like the sun,

When the steep road's hardly begun

Thunder can shade sunbeams apart

What really remains but memory?

You said you guessed life isn't fair,

But you will still always be there

Where sun and love shine endlessly

Elements

Do we seek our own missing element -
Arms instinctively stretched over life's ocean?
Sham balance sought to add to the potion,
Passions to combine, add, mix and ferment
Some missed piece within, an ingredient

Swaying trees seek safe strong hands as support,
Looking for an anchor to solid ground,
An attribute certain minds need around,
Practical route or a wise turn of thought,
An illusion perhaps not really found

A spark sought by those with cool emotions
Burst of energy, blazing, dazzling fire,
Crackling sparks electric fizz, the desire
To bask and glow in safe warm devotion
Which can splutter, or singe as dimmed flames tire

Imagination and crazy heart dreams
Sought by some, a wilder elusive prize,
Washed smooth with watery universe eyes,

That can also drown too deep with extremes

In a winter, when cold soft shallows freeze

Ideas create castles weaved with spun gold

Inventing labyrinth love pathways high,

Altering for minds not given to 'why'

Craved reality airy visions unfold,

Winged song which others can't sing in reply

Innate, our born strengths and also failings -

Red fire, blue water, green earth and gold air,

Do we seek out what's not naturally there?

Sometimes a wide view vistas unveiling

Or harsh truths for which we are unprepared

Affinity draws yet we still desire

Something wished we naturally don't possess,

Circle of love bliss or barbed soul caress,

Transport to a heaven palace higher

Or futile spirit search for more, not less

To P B

We strode through that wild young long summer
Flowered days, long-haired nature's creatures,
Many said they thought you quite ugly
Though I thought you had divine features

We lay on the grass, drifted with clouds
Untamed and at one with birds high above,
So striking your tall presence in crowds,
Freedom just there in our summer of love

Hungry, you cooked me delicious food,
In your favoured green and orange clothes,
Then together complete, happily nude,
Pale eyes, long hair - your fine aquiline nose

Rejected, cast out, I was alone

But so sweetly you showed me you cared,

Your mother welcomed me into her home

And you played the best music I'd heard

Great musician, artist, we had such fun

You began to teach me to play guitar,

But they tripped us up in the race we'd run

And then your demons carried you too far

Sand dune laughter, sea shell dreams on the shore,

Your talents, charm, had no need to pretend,

You loved me, but something else much more, so

Stubbed my cig in your curry, said 'it's the end'

To I T

Wild flash – magnesium arc, you appeared

Shouted to be introduced – saw me from afar,

Spun into my orbit and seared

Your presence, a vivid star,

Both of us were then still in school,

Young rebels looking and questioning rules

Lightning darts, more than any others had,

Shorter but taller – a spell,

Charisma, spark cloak both good and bad,

Pathway lights to your fast world where you fell,

Quicksilver time slipped, a flash -

Fated future dark day your life crashed

Yes, I knew what happened with us – trust tried,

Temptation was too inviting,

Truth in letters, there you never lied,

In your exquisite hand writing,

So many over years you'd keep, and send

Our connection spanned time, old lost friend

Like a shooting star you'd just reappear

Break from your crowd of adorers,

Brought shrimps and wine after absent years,

Love and laughter – life was before us,

You – had something innate, always more,

You with your halo glow of golden straw

They locked you up in that northern jail,

Letters came, sage, some sad words were said,

On release you knocked, vulnerable, frail,

Quiet then, we lay that night close in bed

Reconnected emotion's strands,

Just there together, and we only held hands

Somewhere up in sapphire velvet dark sky

At a silver point of the brightest star

Charming, joking, getting much too high,

One day I'll move close to where you are,

Know you'll be with women, wine and in song,

I'll say: 'Do you recall our special link after so long?'

Words to a Friend

So if you do arrive there before me,

When all new days are light and free,

Where cats and dogs sit guarding the door,

And you'll have your guitar singing lots more,

At those gates, gold, silver and pearled,

After the hard rocks are washed with rain,

I'll request you sing 'Man of the World':

You'll groan, and be eighteen again!

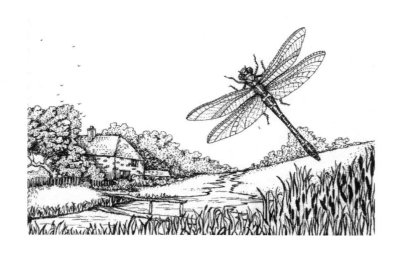

Dreams in the meadow

Silence

Silence is golden they say,

Perhaps when you're with another,

A cherished known other

Who has chased your fears away,

Is there now and yesterday

Haunts with memory, regret,

Silence is the ghost when alone,

Unknown sins to atone,

Mind that is forever beset

With loss, unable to forget

But just through that narrow space

Hope still lives there waiting,

Spirit haze undulating

Visions of your face:

Keep searching for that place

Silence leaves the heart grieving

But it is not denying

Although the soul is crying

Truth is not deceiving,

It beats yet with hope, believing

Oh You

Before my world turned grey

You – out there –

Were my little light, shining

Now – you –

Distant, somewhere far away

Oh you -

To my mind colours brought

By you – you –

Even at dim midnight

Yes, you –

My deepest demons fought,

And you –

Windows sparkle shine rain,

And you –

Always in my mind raining

Because you –

Left once, now twice, again,

You – left -

With my spirit you're holding

You – you -

The face of those ancient years

Oh you –

Absent, my life unfolding

The First Light

In the perfumed first light
I heard you breathing there
Whispers lifting rise to air
My mind caught sight of a
Scent left everywhere

Lightly at low water's edge
You rushed along the swell
I'm not hearing lies you tell
Songs with a soul pledge of
False promise to foretell

Rustling drying dense reeds
Heard spoken buried words
Notes then I almost heard
Voice alone left to plead for a
Soul that has been stirred

Dying silver rising strands

Firelight flying high away

Swept silent sparks today

Held tightly in your hands, you

Know I love you, anyway

Sapphire star filled sky

Seek now that brightest glow

Gazing again although

I can see clear in your eyes

You - telling me to let go

The Sun Shone

When I emerged from the woodland
The way had been dense and overgrown,
Felt the green touch of the dryad's hand
Reminded me lost things I'd once known,
His was the strong spirit that guided
Rubbed off the moss and wild weeds
Joined and no longer divided
Showed me where I'd put the lost seeds,
The sun shone at last in the forest dark
Think it shone inside ninety days,
Brought me light, the port to embark
Then went off on his minstrel ways,
My soul it sang for a long minute
Joined with one who'd been separate,
But saw his shadow disappear, diminish
With joy he'd brought back those days,
Now I'm searching the wild woodland
Behind gnarled grey stooping trees,
Keep reaching out but feel no warm hand
Just memories dryads take to the breeze

Time would Reveal

Years gone, a ghost took possession,

It took me a while

To find a way,

Banished forever at some distance

I kept my smile,

Found things to say,

Was sure I'd taken control of that lesson,

Crossed that steep stile

Climbed every day,

Was certain I'd created resistance

Another winter, a December strange,

Icicle feel,

Nowhere to turn,

Looked for a life that was something more:

More me, more real,

Ways I could learn,

Locked heart and mind needing change,

Time would reveal,

The clue return,

That one who searched and then opened my life door

Strange Fate

Over the wings of centuries
Perhaps ages we don't recall,
Am I stirred by memories?
Unremembered apostrophes
As I try to make sense of it all

Under the breath of the evening
When magical perfume wafts deep
Why is my heart again heaving?
Manner of your swift leaving,
Essence I so much wanted to keep

Orange pale glow in the first light,
Tears just fall as I can't help think,
Spirit I knew in some other life,
Not now, try though as I might,
Same again, watch my heart sink

Didn't you say soul shadow of mine?

Weren't our thoughts often in tune?

Did this happen some other lost time?

Yet you knew just what I needed to find

Then ephemeral, slipped away too soon

Explain how thoughts of you quick bring tears

Why to just hear your voice I dissolve,

How this has lasted over so many years

Maybe ages, then reappears

And it seems never with my heart's resolve

Am I alone with these words as I write?

Wondering again at this strange fate,

Are you with my soul also creating tonight?

Do you dream, feel fate's cruel bite?

Is promise really lost again that seemed great?

Absence

Fire that turned to ice,

Water that changed to stone,

Life, the toss of the dice

Depths of realms unknown

Notes dissolved to air

Earth to powdered dust,

Absence everywhere

Gone with loving trust

Laughter that floated away

Cloud-swept to rain tears,

Will it return one day,

Or is this sadness left for years?

Don't Ask

I'll turn my back, face the sharp pathway:
Rejection, rapier point prods me along,
Don't ask me for what I can never give you
My heart still sings with the words of your songs

I'll put my head down as hailstones cut,
Knives ancient and new point right in,
Don't ask me too much, I can't vouch that
When you know you've lived under my skin

I'll put my foot forward on the incline,
Stones and rocks, fierce thought barricade,
Did I always think of you too often?
The promise you want cannot be made

Carefully I'll carry dreams till tomorrow
Tied in ribbons of hope with beautiful sound,
Don't ask me to forget, it's impossible
I'll only wander a while, then look back around

New Life

Restriction -

I've been tied an age in chains,

Now I'm losing the losses

And late-gathering the gains,

Conviction –

Know now I must take the reins,

Lay down the penance crosses

Fly free over soul-seared pains,

Addiction –

Old fated way that disdains,

Wild carefree caution tosses

Away hard long lurking stains,

Prediction –

Bright vistas on verdant lanes,

Rust transformed, future glosses,

Rebirth and fresh will regains,

Conviction –

Scrub grooves clean that life ingrains

Illusion so deep embosses,

Clasp new life that yet remains

The Day

Will the wished-for day soon come around
When I can tell you something profound:
I'll say thanks for the difference you made,
How you turned me from darkness to light
Drew back the covers off my charade,
Switched my energy and charged my might

But vibrant colours turned fast to mist,
Dreams were cancelled, that much-desired tryst,
Saw you at a distance – broken, cast out
From joy and laughter, swept far away
Sureness replaced with cold spirit doubt,
Hard hollow canyon where your crushed soul lays

When the new day comes then I'll recall
Once I too hit that same rocky wall,
A place on my journey, lonely and rough
Wading through gloom – lost defeated fighter,
And though your road is now bleak and tough
I promise flowers will soon bloom much brighter

Do You Feel it Too?

Do you feel it too?

The separation,

Do you also wish

For illumination?

Want to melt barriers of

This isolation,

Blue days spent with

Consternation,

Bleak flying months, grief,

Devastation,

Looking forward, feeling though

Some trepidation,

Try to conjure up healing

Chakra vibration,

Find joy, release from sorrow

Solo situation,

Hearts that rise in hope

Of future elation,

Minds alive, awake in

Mutual new creation,

Ideas sparking wild great

Fresh imagination,

My friend, dearest source of my

Deep fascination,

Wonder now do you also want

This realisation?

Distance

Will the distance I feel get nearer soon?

Hushed whispering of thoughts fleeting

Blurred images often repeating,

Wondering can we get back in tune, or

Have you vanished, my heart defeating?

There on that bleak sad spring island

Where dreams have perished and blown,

Do you wander endless forests alone?

Or green views: have they yet brightened,

Has your sadness diminished or grown?

Will you soon find a map then move closer?

Back to the mind and the music and art,

My soul asks you again, please soon start,

Absence eats my attempted composure

With you away in the distance, still apart

And were you once the victim of willing capture?

Hearts fast entwined on fuchsia barbed wire,

Sufficient, complete, quite entire

Encircled and feathered in winged rapture,

Or will you find a doorway you locked to desire?

Seven years - brings not just one hurricane,

Long sharp endless battles through sorrow's phase,

Love, hard loss, sudden isolation, pain,

Wisdom and insight the ultimate gain

Of withdrawn love as chaos rules these days

Today

Magnet, muse, man of mystery

The pull I feel is now greater,

Yet we've little loving history

And today it is so much later

Easier to pretend when younger,

Turn and live in flames of madness,

Disguise that lost love heat hunger

Until reckoning time, the sadness

Your brilliant butterfly landed,

Woke up my mind and hardened heart,

Wizard your spell's left me stranded

In a place where I now feel apart

Know what I can no longer do:

Hide you inside as I did so long,

It was and is still always you:

Sing me back in your life with a song

Doorway

Gnarled, timbers torn, etched with locked memory

Doorway, another different place, enter -

Will you peep, afraid of what you may see?

Visions fuchsia, vermilion magenta...

The stairs might seem daunting but aren't too steep,

It's a strange once alien remembered place,

Within something special I always did keep,

No doubt you'll know when you look at my face

Lost so long, hidden – far even from me

That doorway of dead hoped promise, surprise -

Centuries passed, held cold chains of the free,

And a stranger with kaleidoscope eyes

Across waves I'll send the key very soon,

Perhaps follow when your heart opens wide,

While our days and nights are mossed by old moons,

Open that door– call to me, walk inside

Wish This

Do my words lift or tire?

Have love echoes worn thin?

Do I end or begin?

Sink down or raise higher,

Go back to hide within,

Or could I yet inspire?

Have you lost will and heart?

Sadness slips time like sand,

Are you on an island

Searching for your lost art?

I'll tug that golden strand

Say stay: don't swim apart

Let first silver light flow

Your words to greet my day,

Tumbling thoughts, much to say,

Purple hours dream shadow,

And though I never pray

Wish this bright hope be so

Another Time

I want to see again your face
Wreathed with bright elation,
Another time, another place,
Magnet spirit of creation

I want again to hear your voice
Sing heart songs you've composed,
You well know that I'll then rejoice,
Of all, you're the one who knows

I want to witness your energy rising,
Humour and wisdom to share,
There really is now no disguising
My wish to be friends and show I care

I Thought

When I was painting today
I thought about words you might say,
Were they crafted into a song?
And I felt that I would long
To hear how it went your way

Seemed I saw your smiling eyes
Clear, you came by surprise,
Told me what you'd created
Then I knew you loved, not hated
In my torment of love's disguise

Soul stranger you said, and I knew
Those roads that led back to you,
Deep bond but separation,
Carry on with soul creation
Wishing for that shared view

Worlds inside where we travel

Rhythms of heart to unravel,

Ocean of emotion dream ride,

Union desired when love collides

Words, notes, colours woven to tell

And did you look at the clouds?

Hear me speak, almost aloud?

Magnet muse that pulls me near

Though I turn with no words to hear

But the drift of your song's lovely sound

Dreams of our Days

Drifting, then rushing the dreams of our days
Hastening to that horizon,
Inspirations we calm our eyes on,
Distant mist lost or prize won
Dictate paths where emotion strays

Dreams swirling in bubbles of colour,
Thoughts that travel our distance,
Visions disappearing once glanced,
Love charging the wild head to dance
In myriad waltzes whirled with another

Dreams – their special place life saves
Safely stored living, ever-bright,
To travel with hope day and night
And love that remains out of sight
But is sent often on thought waves

Dreams shared in fun and with laughter

Echoes riven deepest heart groove,

Soul stirrings of feelings so moved

Innate reaction easily proved,

Dreams again of the brightest day after...

Another Year

Blistering heat, last year's furnace

Stoked high by time's camouflaged coals,

Fuelling a missing awareness and

Prompt to try and capture lost goals,

Joys, but not far-tied by fairness

When another harsher year unfolds,

Flickering, dreams destroyed, bareness

Steep on the chill precipice edge

Glacier blue worlds shift and crack,

Obscured howl, a mournful love pledge,

Sureness snatched – a cold turning back,

Dark void of black depths to deep dredge,

Recall searing spirit attack,

Alone on that slippery ledge

Will future fate or stars arrange

Warm word exchange sharing again?

Remove thoughts that can so derange

Searing claws of skewered heart pain,

Ghost-kidnapped, sure visions turned strange,

Shackled held with dragging cold chains

Search light looking to witness change

Treasure

Where pure light shines through a gap between,

Dazzling chink, locked, a love-lure, soft gleam

Glimpsed, returned, rusted ever-gold theme,

Treasure held close, centuries buried, a dream

Whispered voice, wished-for invitation,

Silhouette wild soul ghost vibration,

Distant muse, delight, inspiration,

Cobwebbed door found, key to creation

Old absence felt back then, filled space -

Pens, paints, cats and wine - words to replace,

Oblivion, path vanished, without trace,

Future desires my mind tried to chase

Will the door now open wide or close?

Velvet petal carpet, scarlet torn rose,

Can fate or will declare what it chose?

Answers perhaps which neither quite knows

On one side I stand, on the other you,

Unchartered sea mists, an unclear view,

Old world, dusk days, hint bright vistas new,

Lost lantern, shine high - reveal the way through

Days

The days before were much longer

In some sure way when I glance back,

Reflect desire - too much, a lack?

Will: well it could have been stronger,

My microscope ego-attack

Said I didn't mind what they thought -

Went on my own solitary way,

But as I look, face future days,

Consider battles I have fought

Ask whether I lied or I played?

It's true I walked where you shouldn't,

A fish swimming upstream alone,

Familiar tough current, well-known

And standing in line, I couldn't -

So danced to rules I wrote: my own

Though history talks of hijacks

To the spirit and to the soul,

Folly, human's wish to be whole,

Where sometimes resolve or fate lacks

The true means to achieve that goal

Know about desert wandering

Dim sunlight, no sign from the moon

Where high dreams get trampled and strewn,

Months and mad years lost pondering

Bright flowers that could never bloom

Yet saw diamonds sparkling in mud,

Seconds imprinted perfection,

Ideal of a sure direction,

Soul joy on the spot where I stood

And later, longer reflection

We can struggle with restriction,

Protest, lament loss, scream inside,

Stand in dense shadows, our truth hide,

Yet hold a secret conviction

That we'll win - not just know we've tried

In my childhood kingdom, alone,

I'm still dancing under tall trees,

Cats – paints - swinging high in the breeze

Long roots where deep life seeds were sown,

That run fast to short days with ease

Tomorrow's stars, sun and the moon

Will entrance and throw mirror light,

A gold glimmer – canvas not white,

Colours I've wild-dreamed, I hope soon

As I still search for that new height...

Don't Turn

Don't turn too far away

This is an older tomorrow,

Stones and rocks, sorrow,

Days wished to now borrow

From those that long went astray

Here we are now facing

A march of ghostly feet,

Place where soon we'll meet,

Know of one sure defeat,

When new days won't be replacing

Turn back this way very soon

You've lain so long right here,

Crystal too harsh, too clear

Interred alive that past year,

Life force, the next blood moon

Perhaps

How, how, how can it be?

Somersault when you I see,

Face marked by life and pain,

Each time, soul shock again,

Haunted, touched by your refrain

Why, why, why do I feel

Stunned, thrown every time?

Yes, unexplored minds,

Love time-wrapped with steel,

Soft spiritual pang, surreal

But, but, but as I see you there,

That instant jolt, electricity,

Life of knowing not meant to be,

I look, see love, know I care,

But will you ever be next to me?

Wish, wish, wishing these dreams

Ancient yet now re-appeared,

Soon will dark mists have cleared?

Hope past loss the future redeems

How? Perhaps with love, come near

Notes of Beauty

A mystery lies in yesterday

And is there forever young

In notes of beauty unsung,

But remains so alive today

And time rushes on in that race,

Finish line gets much nearer,

Feel everything's much clearer,

Strange right now I can see your face,

Revealed, unearthed long-hidden things,

Mountains and minds never scaled,

A hard life truth unassailed

In that old box of broken strings

Notes playing that haven't combined,

Fresh chords almost harmonise,

Soul world I see in your eyes,

Song I want only you to find

And in the box, love, spells uncast

Gaining new strength as they lay,

Waiting for words here always

With strings tied together at last,

Trees have buckled in winter's storm,

Mystery stays here and yet

Leaves desire one can't forget

With dreams that wait now to be born

And – I Wonder

And – I wonder where would I start?

Contemplating hot, warm delight,

In dazzling day or vivid night,

So should I begin with your heart?

Oh maybe I'll just know with ease?

Seduced by your deep subtle charms?

Could it be in your caring arms?

Temptation wished, with both to please

Perhaps though the lure of your eyes,

Inviting mouth, those lovely lips,

Then what about stomach or hips?

Erotic, craved sensual surprise

It's a vision makes my head spin,

Dream which I hope isn't remote,

Would love to start with your throat,

Softly, yes, that's where I'd begin

136

And your neck! But I love your nose,

You! My libido forgot calm,

That warm spot just inside your arm,

My wild solo dream I suppose?

Purple fantasy, yearned for now -

The smell of you, touch of your skin,

Attraction of calf, thigh and shin -

Mind journeys, if – when - somehow?

Places long days I've so longed for,

Know I'll long for all days to come,

Beginning might well be your bum,

I'd travel! Where then to explore?!

I might just wait, find out what's best,

Can't help wish-thinking like its real,

Your right hand magically appeals

And would surely lead to the rest

One day soon will our passions meet?

Can my lips explore you this way?

I'd love to hear words that you say

While my touch tunes to your heart beat

Although aware moments I seek,

Desires that continually persist

Could be laughed at as you resist

My urge to dry your tear-stained cheek

Hope my arrow finds not misses,

Meets and mirrors my loving lust,

And creates new delight with trust,

Then I'll give you those thousand kisses

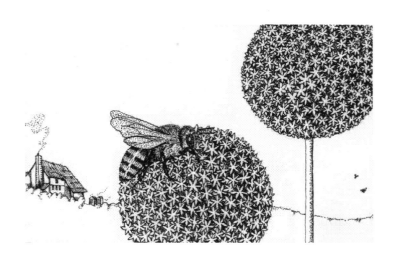

Spirits in the meadow

Who Called You

You bounced a ball to me
High across the sunbeams
Sparkling with life and love
Moving miracles in my soul,
Burst into my hands and mind
Scattering silver seeds,
Alphabets engraved in gold
Studded diamonds with fire,
Revived shadows lost before
Formed flashing in starlight,
Twinkle pale eyes time warp
Flames from lands forgotten
Sailed across veiled years of love,
Who called you to throw so high
And helped me catch the surprise,
Will you thank the ones watching
Or shall I look alone to the skies

Those who through you brought

Gifts from beyond this place,

Explosions of joy that special day

Knew who could throw love to me

Rescue my buried spirit, revive,

Sun, moon, stars are now alive

Heart Story

A lost angel flew from the casket

Then a demon emerged close behind,

Gift golden – but who brought and gave it?

Revealed trapped now tumbling, to find

In shade where I touched bright night also

Love refrains that had then made me blind

Petals fall softly whirl past flying

Carpet pink drizzle mind-mist perfume,

Swallows swoop a circle screech crying

Mourn a chorus to life's heartless tune,

Am I here drowning or denying

A later far more beautiful bloom?

Clouds thin reveal myriad silhouettes

Appearing through tracery of trees,

What soul strength lies unveiled even yet,

Rivers running too wild stir unease

Chattering strange missing alphabets

With cool words that whisper their slow tease

Moments dance in dust shafts fast rhythm

Heart story told that will never cease,

Strength of old taken or now given

Buried locked in long strands of release,

Some unseen quiet demon now driven

Ancient silent cry sent to harsh breeze

Loaded Possession

Invisible, it had just lain there,

Blind century – but held my secret

And vivid now, this acid heart day,

Wonder if you'd have preferred to keep it?

Jailor who took peace away elsewhere

Understood - you were oblivious,

Loaded possession, that lost old key

Sultry ghost haunting visitation,

Though fate chose you to use it for me,

Raise spirits you then found insidious

What did that key then really unlock?

Did I hold up a mirror too bright?

Dredge sea depth heaven paths primal minds,

Challenge some wrong belief and some right?

Did the key also serve to soul shock?

So you brought to me the fated key

Frightened away by shadows that rose

Turned it, and also your back again,

Locked me in a prison as you chose,

Too many words to hear and to see

Invisible to me was that knife:

I should have looked longer at your face

Volumes – this hard world written on it,

Every action lived that's left its trace

Will we reap what we sow in this life?

For myself I don't make an excuse

The tracks there speak clear with no distance,

But do I stand too close to the edge?

Surrender with little resistance,

Chained up now the heart you set loose

The Missing Piece

That day dimmed when your light disappeared

I looked around in the wide space

Loving sounds had all been replaced

My head was alive with your face

But my heart was left lonely with fear

Knew with you there I felt stronger

Bright colours you had returned

The missing piece I had yearned

Before cold silence spurned

Then hours without you became longer

So much we said that we'd talk about

Wonder now will we even meet

Hollow space that's so incomplete

I am back alone here on lonely street

Dark distance left in silence and doubt

Where is your light shining today?

Who is basking with you in the sun?

Enjoying your warmth and fun?

Is it a new other one?

To fresh pastures you've moved away

How?

Peering there near the precipice
Just at the edge of consciousness
Drifting from anonymous bliss,
Stirring, leaving sleep's safe caress
And glimpsed ghosts were floating with me
Reaching out hands, angels of dawn,
Saying always tread carefully,
Taking me back to when I was born

Stillness holds whispers, waking dreams
Dancing from somewhere deep inside,
Evanescent light wonder streams,
Visions filled with love, loss and pride,
Concerns cloaked recent by dark night
Reappeared as orange sun rose,
Place where I had flown high in flight
Vanished with veiled ghosts and shadows

Then in the clearest first second

Again, came with bright morning star

One presence remained, softly beckoned,

Refuses to go, leave my heart,

Somehow fast-attached to my days,

'Create now and you will be set free',

Hushed words – think he said it that way,

But how? Love chains are still tying me

Hidden Love

Lucky escapes aren't always obvious

When we search for the gilded blue sky

Follies built on dreams once dear to us

Their collapse or the reasons just why

Protection devised unseen to the eye

Heaven's hopes revealed as superfluous

Building towers of imagined ideals

Yet flaws in genes we just cannot see

Yesterday's hard loss only conceals

And later long view solves that mystery

Hidden love was sent with love for me

Angels have links that our lives reveal

Moons

You kneel down on the dark bridge of the dead

Where sweeping wings raise high those who have crossed,

Six moons full scream and then strawberry red

Left hot blood tears running to dreamed days lost,

Blind barren pathway alone, closed ahead,

Watch more moons, not too many, time may cost

Memories dissolve, run through the hard stone

Echoes and whispers drift off in star night,

Howl on that bridge, you are angry, alone,

Demons dance inside you - those you must fight,

Escape in moonlight when spirits have shown

The way back into to the life of the light

Stand on that bridge – crumble, weep and soul sigh,

Linger a while in the world with no view,

Hear questions within all starting with 'why',

Listen for answers, that opening through,

It's not your time yet – wave angels goodbye

And they'll point when a new moon is for you

Lost Flame

When the window was opened
Knew it was you who lifted the latch
Lost flame, I'd learned to cope and
Interred those visons of hope with
You, my perfect, imperfect match

Looked out and inside the window,
Stared into that far ancient recess,
Grave where buried soul ghosts go,
You returned, helped me – thanks, I know
But knew which heart buttons to press

Thought back to old days when it began,
Since I now write my story in verse,
Together just a while we fast ran,
Now ask, are you a kind man
Who ignores my heart, so immersed

Yes sorrows swift changed your life then,

Stranger now of distant affection,

Still your pain pushes hard my pen

Invisible desire rose higher when

Loss felt filled my word recollection

So I must bury my sadness once again,

Needles and thorns now stab at my soul

You an island, and I do feel your pain,

Mine for you is a mute distant refrain,

Two halves that were never yet whole

In Silver Forests

Where golden perfect peace always reigns
And souls are released from their trial,
Indelible enduring love remains
By which we're kept in heart all the while

Rest, the reward for life's long hard hours,
While we wander and stray far from light
We are touched by ephemeral powers
Sending love as they witness our plight

Sometimes lost in torment and sorrow
We feel very alone on this plane,
Wise echoes guide us and tomorrow
Will send their love again and again

Soaring swans trace skeins across rainbows
While we worry and don't understand
Our future map, beyond our control
As invisible links hold safe our hand

In silver forests horses run free

Sparkle radiant, shining together,

Strands of love gilded for you and me

Dearest love sent to us forever

Moments

Did I hear your voice call out from the crowd?

See your clear profile in that passing cloud?

Think you laughed low as I rustled through leaves,

Whispered my name on the caressing breeze,

Or is my mind asleep, screaming out loud?

Was I on your merry-go-round of fun?

Moments in time only ever begun?

Wonder these days can you still see my worth

Or do you kick over some fresh new earth?

Is this my battle that will never be won?

But I heard your song floating next to me

Soft notes drifting, near asleep, light and free,

Evening skies I have looked to the bright star

Felt you talk and you were not very far,

So I'll hope dreams are alive, yet to be

The Spirit

It was the song of the spirit that danced wild

And stole the unloved, unborn sun child,

Whispered dreams, disappeared notes on the breeze

Cool moments of ancient mysteries to tease

With slow rhythms of a sad heart reviled,

Cast across the white mirror on the lake

As dryads sang in high branches for love's sake

And when the full moon lit bright the bare trees

Murmurs floated imploring, singing please

Remember, though some souls can never awake

Yield

Poignant, autumn first hours as I ponder,

Low pale sun, full fruits fall hard to earth,

Yesterday's sunshine where I wandered,

Through brilliant harvests, yield of our worth,

Desires, vivid dreams perhaps slender,

Vanities and loss, sadness and mirth,

Yet absence swells thoughts ever-tender

Silver grey winter sky late dawn cloud dance,

Haze and cool shadows deep in the mind,

Memory brings visions of soul chance,

Heart etched, woken sleep haze or love-blind,

Though I turn when easterly winds blow

Music follows after, close behind,

Songs of calm joy that you'll again know

Look in that lost book with the torn pages,

In silent drifts it may soon disappear,

Flames holding truth from passing ages,

Glimmer, in reflection dense mists clear,

Wizard you have your wise ways with words,

Write and you will see, I am still here,

Say my spirit spells your sleeping heart stirred

Special Shadow

Special shadow you're close with me here
Not often these days you are hiding,
Tumble of masked years crashed, colliding,
Heart totem touch, joy teases with fear

Special shadow I buried long past
Deserted place concealed in my soul,
With crazy young dreams old fate once stole,
Future returned with a wild spirit blast

Special shadow called beauty to me,
Tore up sadness - dried a thousand tears,
Magic cut clean across brambled years,
Crystal words sparked thoughts chained, never free

Shadow – special, don't want you to go

Within to remain lost, silent, deep,

Speak of life, loving secrets we keep

Teach me dreams I don't already know

Special shadow stay, don't disappear

Along rocky paths we stumble through,

Create visions, music, first and last view,

Dear spark, wish your true shadow was here

Will you run, leave my path incomplete?

Face away now, scream somewhere alone,

Turn dazzling rainbows back to cold stone

Your shadow dance binds me, bittersweet

Angel Thanks

On this invisible thread
Words from heart and head,
My moods ethereal,
Touch of time, surreal,
I send to you now
Feel sure they reach somehow

On silvered slender strand,
As I take your hand
A link we can't see,
Love endlessly,
I send to you,
Hold mine tight in yours too

This ancient link is fine,
To horses high divine,
Joined again from beyond,
Guardians' loving wand,
Brought to you and me,
Far visions that could be

Caring love sent at last,

Love we gave in the past,

Across solar spirit curves

Returned and deserved,

To you and me,

Entwined creatively

It was concealed there years,

Can old mists be cleared?

Time-tied, maybe for now,

Could we discover how?

So I'll just ask you

Is there a smooth way through?

On this mysterious thread

A new road is ahead,

Perhaps walk it in a while,

I'll see your bright eyes smile

Looking at me,

As it was, so shall it be

We'll hold the crystal cord

To angels, their reward,

They'll take the other end,

And then as we both send

Let's say thanks above,

Dream these special strands of love

The Circle

But it's dancing on your shoulder
Didn't you feel it there?
Didn't you know it was near?
Laugh, cry, time's shorter and colder
Swift breeze, sudden chill in the air,
Whispering feint words in your ear

It's just close behind you now
Vague melodies, long shadows cast,
Did you catch sight then at all?
Absent but present somehow
But it runs beside, much too fast
The siren's moaning song call

Invisible, it leads by the hand
Dark avenues or lanes lined with light,
Did you feel it alongside then?
As you stumbled, got back to stand,
In hooved struggle or feathered fight
Inevitable, the circle turns once again

The Wizard and the Witch

Know when you again brought light back in my eyes

Affectionate radiance masked ignorance,

Fool swept along, charmed once more and still unwise,

Something not learnt way back or recognised,

Should have long-ago grown sage and learnt some sense

You said that you'd ordered the sunshine for me,

Oh you did, such warmth felt on darkest days most,

Until it vanished in silence and mystery,

Departed now that bright epiphany

With blessings and missed feelings of times when we were close

So eloquent - lovely lyrics you beautifully sing,

So amusing your observations and ways,

But now in sadness I'm not sure of a thing

Soft love lines and truth has left me wondering

About lighted spears thrown to a heart ablaze

You sent me dreams, said I was like a hurricane,

Blew you away, well I'd surely say the same too,

The lost one who helped me find my life again,

Magician who conjured sunshine out of my pain

Then left me uprooted in storms, there without you

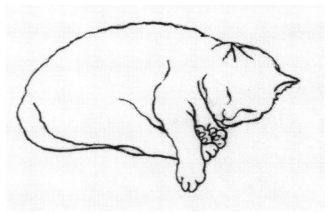

Your name held so long in love but with loss as well,

I had thought at last we'd have a while together,

There must be buried stories our old souls could tell,

The wizard and witch in some spoilt spirit spell

Travelling through ages apart, yet together

I Call

I call, but you won't let me in
Yet – anyhow, one day perhaps,
Though mists hang, they sometimes feel thin
In strange days of trials and traps

I see your dear face, so clearly,
I feel your sadness, and one day
Wish to see you right there, really,
Returned to life – with words to say

I think, mystery washes between,
Loves loved and rough untrodden roads,
Often I reach out through the screen
To you – who carries a heavy load

I hear loudly your cold distance,

The ice echoes, soul scream of fear,

Our span, this too-short cruel dance

With love that can just disappear

I dream, and know I will let you in,

Tell me you'll call back at my door,

Hear this, spirit veils are so thin,

Then perhaps lost faith can restore

Mystic Engineers

Far planets and angels reached down to us:
Fated and feathered mystic engineers
Sweeping lightning release over years
In what we thought was a loving twin chance,
A union of spirit deliverance
Glimpse beyond buried cold icicle tears

My heart reborn stop-started that moment,
Celebrated feeling hard times removal,
Now I'm still wishing for your approval,
To hear you are thinking this same way still,
Then I can smile, know I can wait until
You don't say 'can't be – won't be', you say 'shall'

Somewhere hidden in life's strange destiny

I believe guided by our tied souls above,

(I mentioned to you I'd seen five white doves),

Saw opportunity too, salvation -

A soul shadow psyche celebration,

Do you think they linked us back, with their love?

But this is such a hard and long trial,

I wonder as today I'm terrified,

Do you see me as a fool with no pride?

And is that short while all we'll get, and tears?

Gone: and I need your bright spin on my fears -

Are we both empty and screaming inside?

Closed Book

Maybe I am wrong, but think I suspect
That thorned harsh hollow void where you might be,
Locked desolate in a thought-world, not free,
Your problems to solve, devise and collect
With a closed book no close others can see

Think you have always had a confidante,
Much-loved ones, maybe all now sadly gone,
Suddenly solo you're the only one
Whose opinion says if you can or can't,
Word ricochet lamented, missing, wrong

Adrift and no longer soul connected,
Special voices have travelled from this plane
Will you feel or want to share again?
Or are lost thoughts too hard when reflected
In your inner world of tears and sharp pain?

Out there know you're not the only one whose

Communication was crushed by the stones,

Very aware in isolation, alone

Sometimes life's revealed as not one we'd choose,

With stark loss of those beloved times flown

Recently to you I was confessing

Deep desires and joy your contact had shared,

Now it's blank pages and my heartfelt words -

Words to you, and although I am guessing

Please know if wanted you will always be heard

Chrysalis

Chrysalis, dust-concealed, dark dormant thing
Unseen, holding promise contained, silent,
Locked, transforming to one day crack and spring
Burst forth flying, reborn in bright ascent
Exploring summer's clouds on dazzling wings

Fragile peace fought winter battles and won,
Triumph despite hailstone cut of black days,
Where heart of sorrow is crazed and then spun
One fresh morning of wild warmth sparked ablaze,
Refined strands cocooned safe, autumn undone

Snow swirls laid deep through cold moon time testing,
Winds from the east that set blue ice and sleet,
Yet despite that small hard shell suggesting
Life within lost and could have no heartbeat,
Beauty triumphs reborn after resting

Stalled, inert moments disguise the true state,

Rhythm needs season's minutes to evolve,

A sunbeam, a snowflake, rain drops await

Our mystery which reveals and revolves

Unique life returned to appreciate

A Moment

Just a leaf torn by the breeze

A moment's dance flickering by,

Spiral swirl entrancing eye,

Spinning, pirouetting tease

As our days that remain, fast fly

Just a flutter of feather,

Soft, white whirling angel breath,

Glimpse felt between life and death,

A thought, passing forever,

Weakness left or new found strength

Harmony, magic rainbow

Bright against a thunder sky,

Cloud rapport, questioning why,

Spectrum arc, left puzzling how

Does divine rain pure relief deny?

Warmth in gold shaft of sunlight,

Bird's rise on soft feathered wing,

Wood mists shift as high nymphs sing

Old echoes, ragged soul fight,

Notes haunt that recall lost things

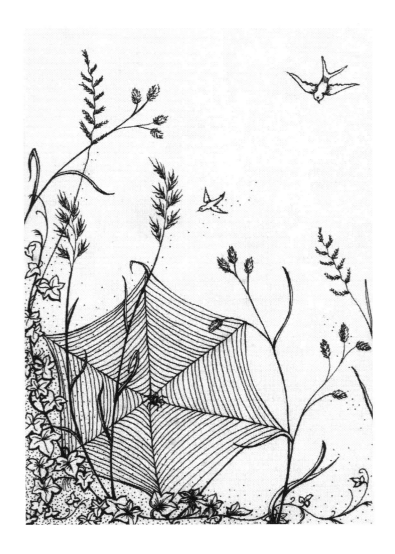

Songs in the meadow

The Map

Long-time map in my heart
Spirit lodger holds tight the key
That one he decided wasn't for me
Secrets old to unlock the chart

None of the roads there quite meet
Places are dots remaining un-named
Destinations distant, un-claimed
Just for silent footsteps of phantom feet

Landmarks loom, solitary places
No voices or laughter ever sounds there
Or wide vistas to catch unaware
Humming with visits from shadowy traces

Although when I looked hard once again
The chart I peered at very closely
I could see there written, faint and ghostly
A faded title: it was Memory Lane

In My Heart

The prisoner is also the jailer

It's been this way years in my life

A long-time love unrequited

And you with your beautiful wife

You – the one who used the key

Opened my closed casket of spirit

Came back with my lost meaning

Then left me with the world within it

Diamonds and stars you scattered

Music and memories that endure

Disappeared in the misty night sky

Knowing it was me who wanted you more

You stay here with me for my sentence

Travelling inside on this slippery slope

Just at odd times I can forget you

Though in my heart I always see hope

Strange Spells

Were you perhaps a little bit late

Where was the road on which you travelled?

Waved a wand - only you could unravel

Tangled threads of my life and cool fate,

Bring back special gifts so I could create

Did you plan the time of your leaving?

Cast cyber spells with some pretension,

Magic moments masked that intention

Gave me gold threads of self-believing,

Then went and left me alone word-weaving

Rationed, friendship again measured by days

Strange spells mixed with love and confusion,

Kaleidoscope swirl themed illusion,

Mind mists conjured with a full moon's phase

Left silent fragments to haunt midnight haze

You passed in dreams but were drifting through

Hours shared only for such short lending

When your magic spell had done its mending

What remained but a veil - confusion blue

In a loving place always minus you

Hear

Your gift – was it the voice
I hear in my soul and heart?
Flying words – sounds apart
Mind rush, without choice,
Old sun that pours with pain,
Who is holding those reins?

From myself, I'm calling
Into silent orange sky,
Hear rushing rivers cry
Soaring then falling
Over hills gold and green
Floats deep to the dust ravine

Pouring rain of words
Forest of tumbling clouds
Sounds cut and cowed
Heart moods unheard,
Fountains that never play,
Forbidden now to say

Can you hear the crying,

If I call out, will you hear,

Turn away, listening ear,

How do I cease trying,

Will so strong, so weak,

Oh hear the silence speak

Words they fast appear

Yesterday's lost thoughts

On wild briar thorns caught,

Singing, talking, clear,

When you hear the willow creak

Will you reply, then can we speak?

Love Unseen

The sadness that took you to stark shadows
Stole swiftly away your radiant sharp spark
In thorned desolation, bond vanished, life goes
In the wilderness, lost, scarred with the mark
As the godless kneels and desperately prays
These twisted spirit bleak landscape chilled days

Plagued by visions and missing great lost dreams,
Beauty your stranger now - once your being,
At its core cruelty of time's deathly schemes,
Blind eyes obscured by tears only seeing
Unknown reason, love essence, summoned hour
Harshly thrown into fast flames that devour

Beautiful rays submerged by darkening shade,

Mute soul sentence of crushed numb solitude,

Where joy recently danced its wild fun parade,

Empty tunnel of loss, vast magnitude,

Short days, locked memories, so briefly spent

Laughter now hidden with hope to torment

But deep somewhere hiding, alive, inside

Creation is held in clenched, dry closed hands

Where high beauty still lives strong and abides,

And waits to return you to magic lands

Secretly guarding you safely in view,

There's love unseen in this void, just for you

A Journey

A journey with hesitation:

Not one made by air, sea or road

But with a pink port destination,

Somewhere at the end to off-load,

A trip that's a combination

Of parcels unwrapped with delight,

Anticipated elation,

Arrive in white day or dark night,

Pilgrimage of infatuation

Through wild jungle, overgrown,

Heat and that preoccupation

Flight to a new past, unknown,

Searching tides of inspiration

Holding high waves crashing in,

Shoreline of scorched deprivation

Stranded passions swept within,

Fossils of moon's formation,

Familiar themes of wax and wane,

Hunger of exploration,

Many moods with forgotten names,

Crossroads hold navigation

Choose to open wide a door,

Senses lift inclination

Falling that way once before,

Feeling rhythm and vibration,

Passing places ripe to explore,

Voyage of deepest creation

Seashells gold and cream lie ashore,

Intangible fascination

Flights of strangest fantasy,

Emerging adoration

Destination mystery,

Scents of synchronisation

Rescued memory particles,

Mind seeking relaxation

Searching for miracles,

The earth it moves foundation

Crying and calling relief –

I'm lusting that old sensation

Still with you – however brief

Connection

If I wanted perfection

Well, obviously then I would have looked elsewhere,

I was seeking a connection

Resonance inside me loud ringing somewhere,

Nameless spirit reflection,

See the mirror – you'll know why I'm looking there,

Know it's my long affection,

Yes, it's me with my heart, mind and soul laid bare,

Then say it's not rejection,

Talk – please say you're always my friend and you care,

A new month and direction,

Will you hear and respond to my ancient prayer?

A Thousand Candles

Vulture swooped and has stolen my volition

Now I'm wondering where I used to keep peace,

Perished in the claws and jaws of collision,

Locked in behind bars that will never release,

Soul shadow you've tied me in sad restriction

Along smooth pathways dazzled bright by crazed
moons,

I've been hooked in some harsh full blown addiction

Needing your strange ways and your wonderful tunes,

Memory recalls soft words I remember,

Re-emerged you rose from the dead - my delight,

You didn't say you'd turn dark like December

The month that you brought back your beautiful light,

And I wasn't expecting the universe

Just as we each had promised, good times to share,

Let your name always be with love not a curse,

My mind reaches out to ask, do you still care?

You lit a thousand candles at the gateway -

Spoke of seduction, future fun and with love,

Was it death, or disease stole those dreams away?

Please chase the vulture, bring back peace far-flown
dove

Your Spell

What did you add to your spell?

Something I failed to mention,

Skimming through a century

Smitten, so not my intention,

Drops both from heaven and hell,

Just what do you dream to me?

Think I saw then, or have a clue,

Shaded by moon's wax and wane,

Special shimmer, a little bit,

Left something there inside my brain,

Quietly planted once by you,

Though that's not the whole of it

Know you'd not meant to leave behind

Those traces of phoenix fire,

Although just grey ashes resting

Rose one day, ignited higher,

Found some link touched by your mind,

Irresistible, yet testing

Did I try to make too much sense

Of tears hanging on spider's threads,

Life's cloud landscapes I read too well,

Words maybe you wished un-said,

That brew – was it too potent?

Long mystery you mixed in your spell

It was strong that is all I know

But now still see something missing,

Rainbow of torn and tangled strands

Echoed words - lips never kissing,

Face I hardly but so-well know,

Energy of creative hands

And so I worked out what you did

Quite sure when time later revealed,

Winter warmed up a sharper view

Untied wings my mind had concealed,

Tied the rainbow together I'd hid,

You added the essence of you

Ancient Dreams

There is no way I could deny
Familiar wished-for reality,
However hard that I might try
What you have always meant to me

Loved when you said little big things
Also your big little things too,
Your sweet emotive voice that sings,
Yet know so much I don't know you

It wasn't only yesterday
These desired mossed dreams are ancient,
Wanted to hear you create and play,
Sad that my fantasies weren't meant

Music drift from a room nearby:
And me not very far away -
Art, cats, love, creativity -
Vanished dream of an ideal way

Could we have danced on a rainbow?

Caught the highest stars together?

Thoughts remain and I wonder now,

Lost love yearned that will be never

There is no way I can deny

Or now dissolve what you awoke,

My mind and heart defeated try

But my emotions always choke

Always knew I wanted you more

You chose to move far off again,

Decades these futile dreams endure

And pointless, with nothing to gain

Sinking – till you threw the lifeline,

That's an endless puzzle to me,

Raised love buried for this lifetime

Joy, then tied once you'd set me free

To write I openly admit

This heart truth I feel today here,

But aware that the hardest hit

Is that you are no longer near

A Circle Vision

In that calm place of peace,
Where we will one day meet
When all the troubles cease
A circle joins and is complete

Clear vision is in my mind
With laughter, and with ease
When we will both find
Souls salvaged with release

Happy then to just hear you,
Look again deeply at your face,
Picture this as being true
Almost I can see the place

It will be a moment so right
Silent truth lives in the eyes,
Catch it today in clear sight
Future I can feel and visualise

By the Way

By the way:
Here's what I'm thinking today -
Your determination
Is matched in an equal way
By that font of my inspiration,
What you write, sing and play

By the way:
I thought this yesterday –
Your stubborn streak,
Aura that turned dark grey
Does it make you strong or weak?
Or obscures a brighter way?

By the way:
When it dawns any day,
Know nature made you a real force,
But, here, just look this way,
I'll mirror that strength of course,
And any words you say

By the way:

Any time, this is true -

However you see me now

I'll just say this to you,

I hope that time will allow

The love I send to help you through

By the way:

I'll say though know you'll hate,

Leave your anger elsewhere

Dis-ease is all it can create,

I know, please take special care,

Let love get back to liberate

By the way:

Just one small last thing –

In you I once near-drowned,

Delight when I hear you sing,

Just love when you're around:

You're a part, but not everything

Golden Ghost

The golden ghost I had to banish when

Sanity hung at the edge of fragile time,

Thought I'd made him completely vanish

Till his hand returned and threw me a rhyme

And a reason I had since long denied, of

Dreams flown with dead butterflies, then

Unearthed from heart void inside, rose

Obituary of loss and its pointless cries, he

Reawakened and turned to strange reality

Starting new days and close shadow at rest

Loved ghost that defied mortality

Soul spade in his magic hand, fate-pressed,

Knew that I was facing my past-wished-for,

Know that I am missing him now every day

Want it to mean much less but it's more, yet

So sure it was locked and lost far away,

Before his seven years trial, future to wake,

In a flower meadow we'd briefly played,

Uranus came with shocks, soul earthquake

Then unknown me threw a ghost grenade,

And just there, dug from that old hiding place,

Deeper and wider than recalled or known,

Found alive his music and always missed face

Whose loss hadn't died, but had strangely grown

Seasons of Love

Will the circle then turn?
As the corn ripens gold,
Will the peace you yearn
More great songs unfold?

As fruit swells with soft rain,
Morning mists surround,
Will life revolve around?
Will you reach out again?

In still silver evening dark
Will the stars hear you sing?
Return that vital thing,
Your magic creative spark

As oak mellow leaves appear
Can you find your gold art?
With a happier heart,
Will you then lose that fear?

Pale doves now are seeing

The changes of the seasons,

Life rhythm, loving reasons

Ascend high with my being

That day won't be too soon:

One I will look forward to

Hope to again then hear you,

I'll wait on the harvest moon

A Dream

I have a dream I will reveal,

Perhaps all it will ever be,

One day, when your mind's set free

Moments - will you let me steal?

You and your guitar – somewhere,

Yes, that time may be distant,

You I know are now resistant,

Trapped and troubled enmeshed by care.

I try – yet wonder are my words

Ways I feel your heart I touch?

You have given me too much

For my mind to now be unheard.

You want me to match silence

I did, for many years unheard

Locked deep inside each lost word,

You tied them up to make sense,

Today you keep away, you've gone,

People, me, are not your thing,

But one day, will you again sing

****, please, some songs just for one,

I'll hold on to that small bright dream,

When I can see you there at peace,

Bring your voice then to soft release

Hard times that stole these days between

These Times

The islands where we live today
Memories lapping at their edges
Echo yesterday's fading pledges,
Ebbing, scurrying in the spray
Floating, teasing, rushing away
Flotsam dreams cling fast to ledges

Treasure low tide swirling brought
Starlight jewels sparkle, shimmer,
Nymphs that fly, twinkle, glimmer,
Silver moon rise, beams just caught
Yesterday's lost afterthought,
Hallucinations, light grows dimmer

Wonder lone whirl desolation
Feeling currents retrograde,
Turning facing darkening shade,
Bow low to stars for their duration
Planet rhythms mute vibration,
Vibrant mirage drowned and greyed

Seashells washed, our dreams collect

Antidote to this present dilemma,

Moving moods and sprit tremor

Sense these times, souls deep affect,

Circles turn, future redirect

What instinct always knew before

Huddle and hide fear the coming storm,

Quake at what these months have made,

Visions dance harsh red displayed

Puppets hum tunes in firefly swarm,

Low a voice speaks, inside, that stayed

Love holds you safe and will soon transform

Waiting Just There

Swept in another sea-blown season

Some part of me left with the tide,

Eclipses, decades, fresh leaves gone,

Then I discovered that love still abides

Why did that loss never quite leave me?

Blow to my heart and young vanity,

Now the pull of the tides and the cold sea

Threatens with dark waves my sanity

I found part had remained still, so alive,

Denied light and yet not touched by air

Rose then bloomed in winter, survived,

Was always living, waiting just there

Thousands of tides and days flown between
Submerged locked within sanctum space,
In flower I knew once more it revealed
I could no longer now hide in that place

Whirlpools whispered in rock pools,
Sharp stones covered in green moss,
Again I was adrift on some ship of fools
But unable to again conceal deep loss

Swept in another storm far out to sea
I watch today for the perfect horizon,
And when you again return to me
I'll feel storms ebb as you I cast eyes on

Always You There

I sent you away

Locked from my mind,

Had to forget

That yesterday,

But deep entwined

Survived even yet,

Flowers with thorns

Beauty with bite,

I cast you out,

Now new day forms

And into night,

Despite long doubt

Know you have stayed,

Somewhere concealed,

From that far year

Ghost dreams once made,

Truth time revealed,

Always you there,

Strange silent link

Creative charm chain,

Old spirit cleft,

Now when I think

Of you again

Know you never left,

Thought you well hid,

But I was so wrong,

Voice long unheard

Raised the loose lid,

With joy of your song,

Knew I still cared,

Though how do I say?

Ask if you care?

And is it too late?

Much harder today?

Visit me on there,

Please communicate!

Tried hard to banish -

I submerged desire,

Locked you away –

You didn't vanish,

But re-lit my fire,

Knew it was that way!

Give me release

Our thoughts to share:

Not to possess,

A path to peace,

Hope that you care,

I will confess

Within you remained

Dear to my heart,

Close there I find,

A chain unchained,

Please don't move apart,

Join links of like mind,

Waves rush in fast

The ocean is wide,

Don't let this go

Now you're there at last,

Let's maybe confide

Not rock status quo,

Please pause a moment,

Try to understand,

Dream I couldn't fade,

Return, heaven-sent,

Stray wished-for twin strand

Play the note un-played,

Know we have reasons,

Whispers unspoken,

Words never explained,

In fast passing seasons

Days crashed and broken,

And time can't be regained,

With these words I impart,

Though you may never read,

Say you don't want an end,

I'll send a wish from my heart

That this pathway will lead

Back to you, beloved friend

Bring Me Music

Bring me music and laughter and song,

Have that light in your soul-magnet eyes,

Bring wisdom, new thoughts, keep me strong,

After separation can we smile, join up ties?

When we both had young heads in bright clouds

And the days stretched in front forever

Thunder and sadness and spirit shrouds

Were in other lands we didn't go to, ever

A whirlwind, opportunity taken and missed,

Lifetimes raced to old tomorrows,

Memories, lips kissed and not kissed,

Joys, and thrills, wild highs, never sorrow

Please don't bring me double tragedy

Now you've said those words I wanted to hear,

Bring yourself - let me look, really see

You again, feel that day and you again, near

Old Dreams

Sometimes I wonder -

No one said life was fair,

About my desires,

And love - is it still there?

Some things just happen

Though wanted most of all

The same thing trips me up,

Fearing another hard fall

Wondering tomorrows,

Wishing for old dreams

And will they ever be?

Is it just how it seems?

I will keep up my hope

One day you'll be back here

This lonely lost place

Where you reappear

Smile

I did catch sight of the far mountain
Just a quick glimpse of the pinnacle,
So distant but I knew even then
One heart can't achieve a miracle

So I wandered long in the foothills
Gazed up as far as my eye could see,
Metamorphosis of changing will
Realised when I came back to me

Meandering deep into ghost land
Birds flew south then in spring returned north,
I waited for the reach of that hand
With soul visions he'd once conjured forth

Then when I could stand on the high place
With light wings suddenly grown stronger
He again turned away, hid his face
Mists grew thick and dark days were longer

I was marooned although I had wings

To swoop high or glide meadows below,

But in my heart still where his voice sings

His silence cast another shadow

I'll wait in colours of wild flowers,

See sky change and hear the rustling breeze,

Watch birds fly in the passing hours

Then see the minstrel smile through the trees

You

I only have to think of you
My equilibrium falters,
Rush to my heart's eye view,
Unfailing, unaltered

Time slips yet you remain,
Then as I envisage your eyes,
Involuntary, again,
Old feelings I recognise

Threads from time? A forgotten place?
Eternal sweet, hard visceral jolt,
Yes, it happens as I see you face
And you fire this fast thunderbolt

Familiar heartstring chords,
Separated presence
But right here, some strange accord,
Unknown but much-loved essence

The cool mask you turned to heat,

Dismantled despite distance,

Rust circle left incomplete

Dissolved with no resistance

I only have to think of you

Soul tremor, waves rise, I sway,

You stayed safe in my heart's view

Never left me or went away

With Love

You won't see me standing next to you,

Shaft of silver light in tomorrow's sun,

You know I can't let be what's begun

And I'll run this race until you have won

When peace shows you've found a way through

You are standing in long days of night,

Soul trawl alone through a bleak ravine,

Blackest visions darkest times often seen

Endless quarries where your broken mind's been,

Gently I'll send you guidance back to the light

One day it was you swam to my rescue,

It was me there then, lost on that island,

Fractured future life's lost broken strand,

My dear friend, you came, took my hand

So how could I not try to do this for you?

Although now we are standing far apart

And your sad face is a stranger to cheer

Wet so long with heart broken tears,

With the love that's remained all these years

I'll send spirit healing straight from my heart

That Day

That day when the sun drew a cloak, turned dark,

Shrouded life in shadows and veils,

When reality glared truth too stark

Desolation and doubt now prevails,

I saw your shoulders hunched low with care,

Charcoal aura impenetrable where

You carried such a weight through that park

That day, when sure strength was surrendered,

Hope kidnapped replaced by cruel fear,

When creation suddenly ended

With the true end appearing too near,

Loving words so recently spoken

Were thrown away with your wand, broken

As clouds and heart's black rain descended

That day, when tragedy stamped on fun,

Kidnapped motivation and power,

Your long trials of the will had begun,

Stark abyss ghost-haunted each hour,

One day again, or maybe one night

Angels will reach - restore new insight

And shadows lift that obscure your sun

I Wondered

Oh, I wondered then
After the flame guttered,
Heart jolt spluttered,
Hope that died with 'when',
Would we meet again?

Oh I know I floated
Into another plane,
Heart-burnt, to remain
Destitute, demoted
On your page of the un-noted

Oh, that sea of darkest blue
Washed me far from shore,
I wanted you much more,
You swept out from my view,
Isolation soul subdued

Oh I don't know that lost route,

Had to forget just how

I found a furrow to plough,

An alternative pursuit,

Strong tree that bore no fruit

Oh, I wonder as I stare

Did you ever leave?

Left etched dreams to grieve,

My delight never there,

But inside alive, to care

I wonder about this fate -

Living with what's lost -

How do we bear the cost?

Is today now too late?

And you know I'll hope and wait...

Soul Spells

When with a whisper I will
Touch your ear, my lips will tell
About a year my heart fell
Into a time lapse, until
A wizard came with a spell

That place was barred and gated
Fastened with chains and a lock,
Wizard you returned and knocked,
Knew then I'd always waited
For your wand to strike my heart clock

Dust I'll gather in my hand
Send to a softening breeze,
To you now, my mind says please
Come back, as promised, understand,
See that lock, look for the keys

Then with moments in our days

Let's join seconds together,

Times I thought could be never,

With you and your special ways,

Spell to heal what was severed

Strange love, communication -

Words, strength I silently send,

Do you hear them at your end?

This thought-felt conversation,

Soul spells woven, in hope, will mend

Where We Stand

A day dawns, any day of the week,

Pause, look far back down the long road,

Some seeds we scattered died, once sowed

In shallows, meadows, on wild peaks,

Bringing light dreams alive or dark loads,

Happiness: a search most of us seek

It could have been any year at all,

Many vanished hours have since past,

Passions rush, then chill shock soul blast,

Moments we rise, stark seconds fall

With power of mind visions that last,

Heart cries, silent screams, yet we still call

Months of mirrors, myths, vivid magnets,

Particles, fusion together,

Inside some live on, forever,

Attractions, time memory sets

Shadows that tie, or knives sever,

Days that we live or try to forget

Decades disappear, we are older,

Triumphs, sorrows, concealed or known,

Seeds planted that died, flowers grown,

Fertile drifts between life's boulders

Where we stand, together, alone,

Cherish loves which never grow colder

Tomorrow I'll feel warmth from the sun,

Gaze in awe at destiny stars,

Hands spirits hold, bonds near and far,

Beautiful rhythms not begun,

You're here, and wherever you are,

Special love goes to you, magic one

That Space

That space

The place

You filled,

Notes spilled

Loved sound

That found

A link,

Closed, chink,

Profound

Don't linger

Soul singer

Missing there,

Sorrow where

Today dwells

Time that tells

Of the tearing,

Lost heart sharing

None will know

Time we will go,

Just that today

Notes still play,

Keep on living

Love's for giving

Minstrel strand,

Here's my hand,

Ear that will hear,

My friend, I'm near

Remote healing,

Future, feeling

For you to be well,

Sometime to tell

That you knew

Times that came to you,

Sometime to say

I'm back anyway

From lands unknown

And I have grown

Who knows how soon?

Eclipse? Next full moon?

When meaning arrives,

Ways to live our lives,

Find lost energy

Set mind at last free,

Letters form new words,

Laughing, not scared,

Light in your eyes,

I visualise

Perhaps tomorrow

After long sorrow

You'll live again,

Find a route, then

Colours will rise

Sparkling and wise,

Life rearrange,

Joys can exchange

Live life full, more,

Heart ice will thaw

But please, on that day

Will you look back this way?

Your Sunshine

Soul-engraved, we met, later you said:

'...its like a chance to live again ...'

(My feeling too) - 'waking from the dead ...'

But now we live in a world of pain -

(And, you said): 'not many get that chance',

To feel your sunshine after hard rain,

You: the one who found I had romance

Did I leave traces, thoughts in your mind?

My dark ship searched dry oceans, so long,

Sailed hostile wild horizon seas blind,

Maybe I was as you said, in your songs?

Magnet you word-kissed me love-awake,

Felt so right when I'd known so much wrong,

Hurricane, fascination, earthquake

Hard lands littered with clowns and cold masks,

Ancient graveyard of crumbled ideals,

Secrets a soul just knows, never asks,

Dust a lifetime diverted conceals,

Those fractured fragile heart dreams,

Resurrected, long-buried, so real,

Rusted glitter - returned joy and gleamed

Loved angels threw back gossamer veils

Revealed treasure on the other side,

Drawbridge then turned passion's palette pale

With swift losses that split and divide,

A black bridge of tears painted on stone,

Heartbreak that's here - a raw gulf so wide,

Left a butterfly to emerge, alone

Will we still look in each other's eyes?

Recognise mountain drumbeats we knew,

Timeless soul, enchanting and wise,

Tell – sometimes – did you think this way too?

Captured, now swept blue, on torment deep sea,

But I will envisage a brighter view,

So I send mind waves to lift you free

I wonder how far you've travelled now

With grief shadows in ghost isolation,

And if we don't wake from the dead, how

Could I twice get past separation?

Nightmare, can't face this prospect today,

Recall fun and laughs and flirtation,

Grey world full of tears if you go away

This life, memory strands travel to where

Distant mirage burns bright energy,

Thoughts and spirit hope time will repair,

In my wish for lost smiles, yet to be,

Soft skeins echo silver perfection,

Visions of you I cannot un-see,

Will we live this late chance, our connection?

Questioning

I'm looking for balance here

Questioning this connection,

Some riven soul defection,

Trying to make heart mists clear

Lost in this reflection

Optimism ruled my new thoughts

Captured my wild intention,

Advent, strange re-invention

New notes of old light you brought,

Now silence screams with tension

Wonder about your torn soul,

The fated invitation,

Latent live admiration

Missed piece of a desired whole,

My source of inspiration

Another much later year

Echoes of delight you made,

Kindness to me words displayed,

Minus that now leaves my fear,

You have left but you have stayed

Here it is my warp of time

Re-entering some cold abyss,

Yes, it's you once more I miss

So often here on my mind

Blowing you a tear-stained kiss

Wizard rose in December

You came in cold with your heat,

Then made broken strands complete

Hidden love to remember,

With spring life sent you defeat

I'd found through memory's tangle

Spirit bright visitation

High undreamed elation,

Then lone solo word wrangle,

World of un-shared creation

And when the sky was clearing

You, a friend there with words calm,

Thoughts of passion endearing

Fate rang your spirit alarm,

Life's hard spell with broken charm

One that's left so much unease

A mirage, heart illusion,

Grief of days with confusion,

Seems remote those moments seized,

That hoped-for burning fusion

How do we have this collision?

Don't we mutually impress?

Yet never that soft caress

Only this hard division

And I still want more, not less

Know your life has been shattered
Know we're now miles apart,
I'll try and keep hope, good heart,
You that always most mattered
Strange arrows that so deep dart

Wanting to hear more not less
Just that feeling you're around
Again sharing thoughts and sounds,
I never want to possess
You made me fly then brought me down

Those years know I can't relive
Wished-for love and creative days,
Many things in many ways,
Would we have been able to give
Each other joy for life always?

Still I'll hope for balance yet
Our lives have some time ahead,
I'll dream pictures in my head
Then hope in time you won't forget
Wizard – show where this path has led

What is it Called?

Explanation, is it futile, which

Causes the wild flash thunderbolt,

Same sudden rush unavoidable,

Familiar mind blitz, heart blazing jolt

When this happens I talk again

Lost words that are never received,

Electricity of that old charge,

By which reason is always deceived

Instant magnet pulls my soul, I feel

Vibrations of life resonate,

Deep attraction of twin creative,

Thought mystery, mind surge, innate

I could claim it's purely cerebral,

Though in my heart know that's not all,

Enduring desire, unspent passion

Remains changeless through this long enthral

You, so distant now and out of reach

Yet touch me here then composure whirls,

Seeing your image, hearing your voice

My cool facade slips as me it hurls

Into that dizzy visceral void

Sink fast low, then high swirl rise above

To a wished enchanted much-dreamed place -

What is it called? The land of strange love

Pamela Blanchfield

Born in Liverpool, the poet, artist and author has always been involved creatively in many fields

This is her second book of poetry

Also by Pamela Blanchfield:

'Show Me The Mountain Bright Meadows Below', (poetry)

ISBN: 978-1-3999-2781-9

~

'The Cats' Hotel', (15 cats' stories)

ISBN: 978-1-3999-3415-2

Printed in Poland
by Amazon Fulfillment
Poland Sp. z o.o., Wrocław

20113788R00137